Protecting Habitats

Polar Regions in Danger

Anita Ganeri

W

FRANKLIN WATTS

LONDON•SYDNEY

Designer Rita Storey
Editor Sarah Ridley
Art Director Jonathan Hair
Editor-in-Chief John C. Miles
Picture Research Diana Morris
Map artwork Ian Thompson

© 2004 Franklin Watts

First published in 2004
by Franklin Watts
96 Leonard Street
London
EC2A 4XD

Franklin Watts Australia
45-51 Huntley Street
Alexandria
NSW 2015

ISBN 0 7496 5816 9

Printed in Hong Kong/China

Picture Credits
Klaus Andrews/Still Pictures: 25
Fred Bruemmer/Still Pictures: front cover
b, 12
Stuart Donachie/Ecoscene: 16, 23
Bryan Knox/Ecoscene: 14
NASA/Ecoscene: 21
Graham Neden/Ecoscene: 4
Fritz Polking/Ecoscene: front cover t, 10,
15
Galen Rowell/Corbis: 1, 19
Kjell Sandved/Ecoscene: 22
Roland Seitre/Still Pictures: 8
Roger Tidman/FLPA: 7
Robert Weight/Ecoscene: front cover c, 24
Mike Whittle/Ecoscene: 26

Every attempt has been made to clear copyright.
Should there be any inadvertent omission, please
apply to the publisher for rectification.

Note to parents and teachers

Every effort has been made by the Publishers to ensure that the
websites in this book are suitable for children, that they are of the
highest educational value, and that they contain no
inappropriate or offensive material. However, because of the
nature of the Internet, it is impossible to guarantee that the
contents of these sites will not be altered. We strongly advise that
Internet access is supervised by a responsible adult.

CONTENTS

What are the polar regions?

Lying at both ends of the Earth, the two polar regions – the Arctic and Antarctic – make up about 8% of the world's surface. Covered in vast expanses of ice and snow, and battered by gale-force winds, the poles are among the Earth's most isolated and hostile habitats.

The Arctic

The Arctic is centred on the North Pole which marks the northern end of the Earth's axis. The region includes the Arctic Ocean and the northern parts of North America, Europe and Asia, together with the island of Greenland. Some geographers describe the area as the Arctic Circle, an imaginary line

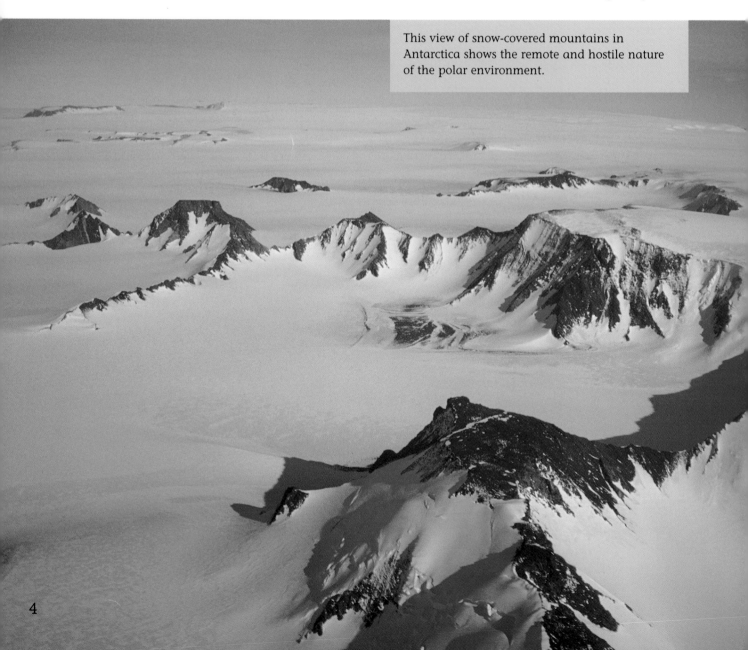

This view of snow-covered mountains in Antarctica shows the remote and hostile nature of the polar environment.

UNDER THREAT

Today, the polar regions are under serious threat. Pollution, drilling for oil, mining, overfishing and illegal fishing, tourism and other human activities are damaging these fragile habitats and putting their people, plants and animals at risk. Scientists are worried that changes in the polar regions will have a knock-on effect for the rest of the world. This book looks at some of these problems and the measures being taken to protect these special places and safeguard them for the future.

drawn around the northernmost part of the Earth. The name Arctic comes from the ancient Greek word for "bear" and refers to the star constellation of the Great Bear which appears in the northern sky.

The Antarctic

The name Antarctic means "opposite the bear". It is used to describe the region around the South Pole which marks the southern end of the Earth's axis. The region includes the continent of Antarctica and the sea around it, which is called the Southern Ocean. It is bordered by the Antarctic Circle. The fifth largest continent, Antarctica is also the most isolated. Its nearest neighbour is South America, 1,000 km away. The last continent to be mapped, people did not set foot in Antarctica until almost 200 years ago.

Polar cold

Both of the polar regions are among the coldest places on Earth. The poles are so cold because the Sun's rays hit them at an angle and are spread out over a wide area. Additionally, the rays have to take a longer route through the Earth's atmosphere to reach the poles and much of their heat is absorbed on the way. The vast covering of ice at the poles also helps to keep them cold. Instead of soaking up the Sun's rays, the white ice reflects most of the heat back into space. This is called the albedo effect: light colours reflect heat away, while dark colours absorb heat.

In Arctic Greenland, winter temperatures plummet to below –40°C. The Antarctic is even colder, with an average winter temperature of –60°C. Even in summer, temperatures inland rarely rise above –15°C. The lowest air temperature ever recorded on Earth was measured at –89.2°C at Russia's Vostok research station in Antarctica on 21 July 1983. As well as being the coldest continent, Antarctica is also the windiest, with wind speeds of over 300 km per hour. At both of the polar regions, the wind makes it feel colder than it actually is. This is called the wind-chill factor. It means that every 2-km-per-hour increase in the wind speed is equivalent to a drop of 1°C in temperature.

The ends of the Earth

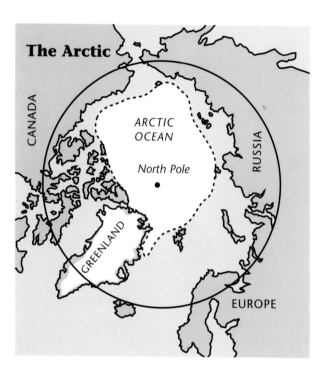

The Arctic

CANADA

ARCTIC OCEAN

North Pole

GREENLAND

RUSSIA

EUROPE

The Antarctic

ANTARCTICA

South Pole

SOUTHERN OCEAN

The Arctic and Antarctic have many things in common. Both are cold and icy, with short, cool summers and long, dark winters. Both are remote, and hostile. Yet there are big differences between the polar regions, too.

Frozen ocean
There is no solid land at the North Pole itself. It lies in the middle of the Arctic Ocean which, for most of the year, is covered in a layer of permanently frozen ice up to 3 m thick.

Covering about 14 million sq km, the Arctic Ocean is the world's smallest ocean and is almost entirely surrounded by continents and islands. These include Greenland, the world's largest island. Much of Greenland is covered by a huge sheet of ice up to 3 km

thick. The low-lying, ice-free land around the edges of the Arctic Ocean is called tundra, which comes from the Finnish word for "treeless". Strong, icy winds sweep this region, making it impossible for tall trees to grow. Beneath the surface, the ground is permanently frozen. This "permafrost" can be up to 600 m thick and even in summer only the top few centimetres thaw. The tundra is dotted with lakes and marshes because the permafrost stops water from draining away.

Icy continent
In contrast to the Arctic, the Antarctic is a frozen continent surrounded by sea, with the South Pole roughly in the middle of it. The continent of Antarctica covers about 14 million sq km, as big as the USA and Mexico combined. It is also the highest continent on Earth, with an average height

For several months during the summer, the Sun never sets in the polar regions. During winter, the opposite happens and there is 24-hour darkness.

This happens because, as the Earth orbits the Sun, it spins once on its axis every 24 hours. The Earth also tilts on its axis so that one hemisphere leans towards the Sun while the other leans away. While it is summer at the North Pole, it is winter at the South. So, while the North Pole has constant daylight and the Sun shines even at midnight, the South Pole is cloaked in darkness and the Sun never rises above the horizon. Then the seasons are reversed.

above sea level of 2,300 m. Over 99% of Antarctica is capped by ice (see pages 10–11). Buried beneath the ice are mountains and volcanoes, including the active volcano, Mount Erebus. The tops of the highest mountain chains stick up above the ice. Less than 1% of Antarctica is free from ice and snow. Much of this is made up of vast areas of bare rock called "dry valleys". Technically, Antarctica counts as a desert because it receives only 150 mm of rain or snow each year. Astonishingly, the dry valleys near McMurdo Sound in southern Antarctica have had no rain for two million years.

The Arctic Ocean is frozen for most of the year.

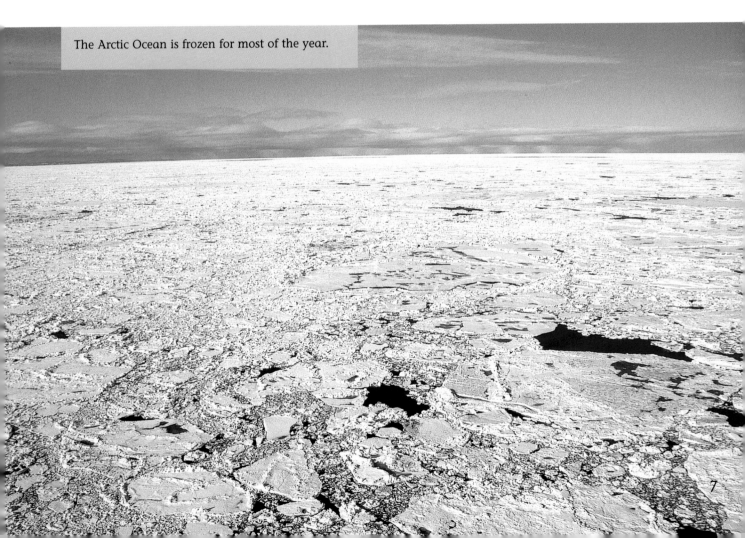

Why are the poles important?

At first sight, the polar regions may seem desolate, ice-bound wastelands. But, because of their position at the ends of the Earth, they are vitally important to our world. For instance, the poles help control weather systems, and provide rich environments for scientific exploration.

Science laboratory

Because they are so clean and unspoilt, the Arctic and Antarctic are exciting places for scientific research which cannot be carried out anywhere else on Earth. At both poles, scientists are using the latest, cutting-edge technology to find out as much as possible about polar geology, climate and wildlife.

Research carried out at the poles is not only important for life on planet Earth. Scientists in Antarctica have found colonies of bacteria flourishing in some of the harshest conditions known. The bacteria live in pockets of water buried 2 m beneath the ice. They use tiny amounts of sunlight, carbon dioxide and minerals for nourishment. In winter, they can even survive when the water freezes solid. These findings have made scientists wonder about the possibility of life existing at the polar ice caps on planet Mars, where the cold, dry conditions are similar to those in Antarctica.

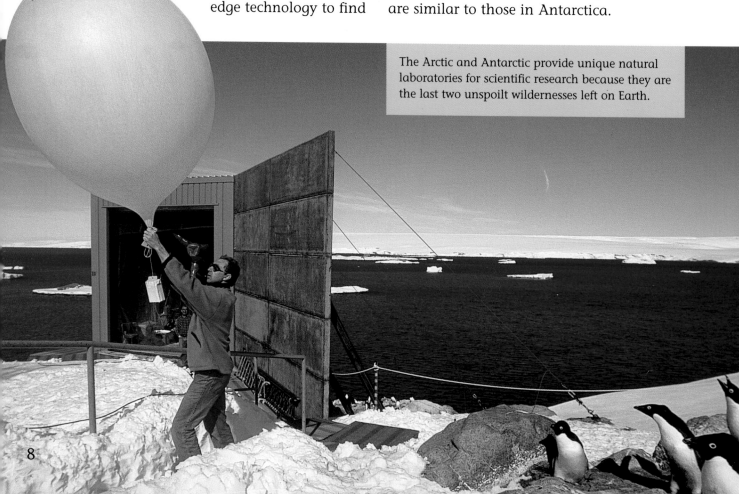

The Arctic and Antarctic provide unique natural laboratories for scientific research because they are the last two unspoilt wildernesses left on Earth.

Global climate

Because the poles are cold, they play a vital part in regulating the world's weather and climate. The cold, icy ground at the poles means that the air above it is always cold. This cold air sinks and spreads out from the poles, creating an area of high pressure. Meanwhile, warm air at the Equator rises, causing an area of low pressure. Air moves from high to low pressure, causing the world circulation of winds. The winds spread heat around the Earth, regulating its temperature. Where cold polar air meets the warm tropical air, it creates weather systems and storms. Without the poles, we would not get these weather systems.

Polar weather is so important for the rest of the world that it is a major area of study for scientists. In Antarctica alone, there are about 100 weather stations. The information they collect is sent to weather forecasting centres all over the world. Scientists think that the world is getting warmer, putting the polar ice caps at risk. If the ice melts, it could raise sea levels by many metres and spell disaster for low-lying areas (see page 20).

Polar resources

It is thought that large amounts of precious oil, gas and minerals lie buried beneath the poles. In the Arctic, people have already begun to exploit these resources by building oil pipelines and refineries. But scientists are worried about the effects of pollution and damage to the fragile polar habitat. At present, mining and drilling for oil are banned in Antarctica for at least the next 50 years. But as the world's population grows, so does pressure on the Earth's resources.

THE ANTARCTIC TREATY

The Antarctic Treaty

No one owns Antarctica, but in 1959 12 countries signed a document called the Antarctic Treaty, aimed at safeguarding Antarctica for the future. Today, 44 countries have signed up. This is a summary of the Treaty:

- Antarctica shall only be used for peaceful purposes.
- Scientists will have freedom to work.
- Scientific information will be freely shared among all the countries with bases in Antarctica.
- All territorial claims will be set aside.
- Nuclear explosions and the disposal of radioactive waste are banned.
- The Treaty applies to the land and ice shelves but not to the high seas.
- All bases, ships and aircraft operating in Antarctica must be open to inspection by any other Treaty country.
- People working in Antarctica must abide by the laws of their own country.
- Treaty countries will meet regularly to discuss new ways of improving the Treaty.
- Treaty countries will try to make sure that all activities are in keeping with the Treaty.
- Any disputes will be settled by negotiation, or by the International Court of Justice.
- If all countries agree, changes may be made to the Treaty at any time.
- The Treaty is open to any member of the United Nations, or to other countries invited to join.

Ice cold

The landscape of the poles is dominated by ice. Because of the bitter cold, the snow that falls on the land rarely melts but settles in layers. The weight of each new layer presses down on the layers beneath, packing them down until they turn into ice.

Sheet ice

Over 99% of Antarctica is covered by a gigantic ice sheet. The largest single mass of ice on Earth, it contains about 30 million cubic kilometres (cu km) of ice and about 90% of the world's fresh water. The ice is so heavy that the underlying land has sunk below sea level beneath its weight.

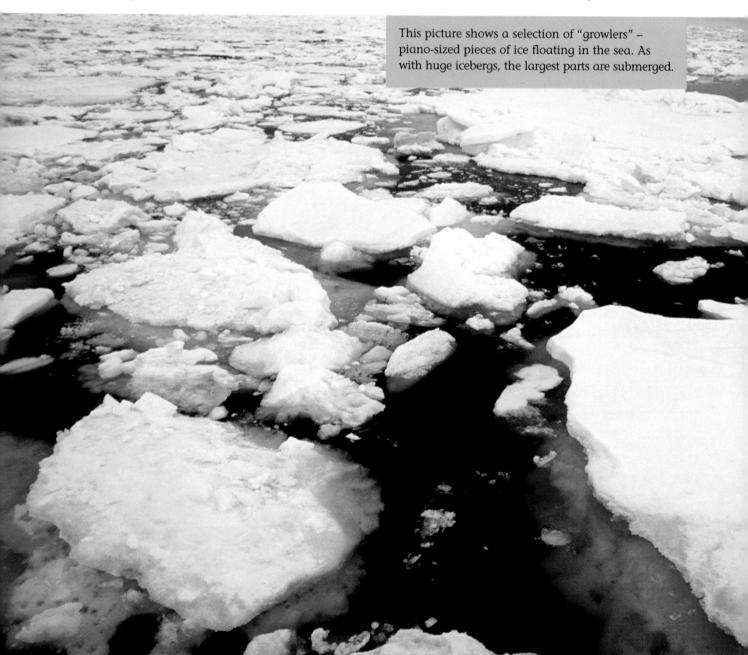

This picture shows a selection of "growlers" – piano-sized pieces of ice floating in the sea. As with huge icebergs, the largest parts are submerged.

On average, the ice is 2,450 m thick. At its thickest, it reaches almost 5,000 m and is millions of years old. Most of the Arctic island of Greenland is also covered in a vast ice sheet up to 3,000 m thick. The ice sheet measures 2,500 km from north to south, and 1,000 km from east to west. It contains over 4 million cu km of ice.

Glaciers and icebergs

Under the force of gravity, ice from the centre of the ice sheets flows towards the coast in frozen rivers called glaciers. In places, these float out to sea as massive ice shelves. Each year, thousands of chunks of ice break off the glaciers and ice sheets to form icebergs. They vary in size from small "growlers" the size of pianos to towering bergs as tall as ten-storey buildings. Nine-tenths of an iceberg is hidden underwater.

About 15,000 icebergs break off the Arctic glaciers each year, mostly from Greenland. Arctic icebergs are usually craggy and melt before they are two years old. Antarctic icebergs have flatter tops and are much bigger – the largest iceberg ever seen was the size of Belgium. They can survive for ten years or more. The wind and ocean currents can carry icebergs for thousands of kilometres from their source. Arctic bergs have been reported as far south as Bermuda.

Frozen oceans

When the sea freezes, it forms a type of salty ice called sea ice. The Arctic Ocean is covered in a year-round layer of sea ice, between 5 and 7 m thick. The extent of the ice cover varies with the seasons, expanding in winter and melting back in spring and summer. The sea around Antarctica is frozen for most of the year. The ice reaches its greatest extent in September, when it covers about 20 million sq km of the Southern Ocean, more than doubling the size of the Antarctic. The ice is about 1 to 2 m thick. Nearly all of the sea ice melts back again in summer.

The wind and waves keep the sea ice constantly on the move. They also break it up to form pack ice. Individual pieces of pack ice are called floes, and range in size from a few metres to more than 10 km across. As the ice drifts, cracks and channels open up in it and the floes pile up on top of each other. This makes conditions very dangerous for ships.

This cross-section of Antarctica shows the thickness of the massive ice cap (blue) contrasted with the area of solid land beneath.

Animal adaptations

Despite the harsh conditions, a surprising number of animals, birds and plants are able to live in the polar regions. They have many special features and ways of behaving to help them survive the bitter cold and biting winds. Among these amazing animals are many that brave life on land.

Ice bears

Polar bears live along the Arctic coast and on the sea ice, where they often float for hundreds of kilometres on ice floes.

These massive hunters are well adapted for life in the harsh Arctic climate. Their thick, oily fur helps to keep them warm and waterproof. A layer of blubber, or fat, underneath their skin adds extra warmth

and acts as a valuable food store when the bears' main food of seals is scarce. When there is little food about, the bears will also scavenge on whale, seal and walrus carcasses, and even steal food from human settlements.

Polar bears are usually solitary animals, except during the breeding season. In December or January, the female digs a warm den in the snow where her cubs are born. They stay in the den until spring, feeding on the female's rich, fatty milk.

Arctic animals, such as these polar bears, are specially adapted to the extreme conditions in which they live.

Cunning camouflage

The adaptable Arctic fox changes its coat according to the seasons. In summer, it grows a thin coat of grey-brown fur. This helps to camouflage the fox among the tundra rocks so that it can creep up unnoticed on its prey of small mammals and birds. In winter, the fox grows a thick white coat which keeps it warm in temperatures as low as –40°C and camouflages it against the snow. Another adaptation to the cold are the fox's small, round ears and nose. These help to cut down on heat loss from the fox's body and make it less likely to get frostbite.

Antarctic animals

Very few animals are able to survive all year round in the cold, dry and windy climate of Antarctica. Many animals, such as penguins and terns (see page 14), are summer visitors who come to Antarctica to take advantage of the safe breeding sites along the coast and the plentiful food supplies to be found in the Southern Ocean. But most of these animals leave again when the hostile winter weather draws in. Only a few tiny insects and other invertebrates can live permanently on land. These include microscopic mites, worms and springtails.

Antarctica's largest year-round resident is a flightless midge, just 12 mm long. These animals spend their lives hidden among the tangles of mosses and patches of gravel and wind-blown sand. They have developed an amazing range of techniques to stop their bodies from freezing in the bitter cold. They have a special chemical in their blood which acts like anti-freeze in cars. The females lay eggs which can survive the worst times of the year in case the adults die. The midges also lose all the water from their bodies and shrivel up when the temperatures fall. This prevents crystals of ice forming in their fluids and damaging their body fluids and tissues.

One of the reasons for the lack of land animals in Antarctica is the small number of plants. Plants start off all food chains and animals cannot survive without them.

CARIBOU JOURNEYS

Caribou, or reindeer, visit the Arctic in summer when the weather is warmer and food is plentiful. In spring, huge herds of caribou travel along the same migration trails they have used for years, heading north to the tundra. Here they feed on lichens and other plants. As winter approaches, they gather to travel south again to their wintering grounds in the northern forests.

For centuries, Arctic people, like the Sami, have relied on these animals for food, fuel and materials for making clothes, tents and tools. Today, however, the caribou and their journeys are under threat as their habitat shrinks and oil-pipeline construction destroys their traditional migration routes. Another danger is pollution, which is contaminating the lichen that the caribou eat.

Birds of the poles

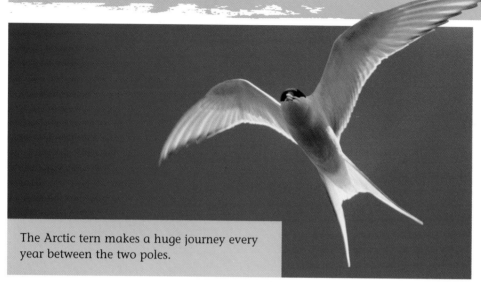

The Arctic tern makes a huge journey every year between the two poles.

The polar climate is too harsh for many birds to survive there all year round. But in summer there are rich pickings to be had on the Arctic tundra and in the seas around Antarctica.

Many polar birds are summer visitors who travel long distances to feed in the Arctic and Antarctic regions. Many seabirds also come ashore to find places to breed.

Keeping warm

Many polar birds share similar adaptations to polar animals. They are well protected against the cold, with dense, fluffy feathers and thick layers of fat under their skins. The ptarmigan is one of the few year-round residents of the Arctic tundra. It feeds mainly on leaves and berries. In winter, its pure white plumage hides it from predators among the snow. To keep warm it burrows into the snow, out of the biting wind. As summer comes, the ptarmigan changes colour to brown so that it is still well camouflaged.

Endless summer

Each year, the Arctic tern makes a record-breaking journey to spend summer at either end of the Earth. During the Arctic summer, it breeds around the shores of the Arctic Ocean. Then it flies south to Antarctica to take advantage of the rich summer food supplies. On each round trip, a tern flies non-stop for eight months and covers 40,000 km. No other bird makes such a long journey. Most terns fly over the sea, feeding as they go. By making such a large migration, the tern spends most of its life in daylight.

Winter breeders

During the cold winter months, most birds leave the Antarctic and head for warmer places. Hardy Emperor penguins, however, breed on the ice in mid-winter. The female lays a single egg, then spends the winter at sea. Meanwhile, the male incubates the egg. He carries it on his feet, tucked under a warm flap of skin.

For the next two months, in temperatures below –40°C and with winds gusting up to 200 km/h, the male hardly moves and cannot feed. He and thousands of other males huddle tightly together for warmth. By the time the female returns to feed the chick, the male has lost half his body weight. Then it is his turn to go to sea and feed.

WANDERING ALBATROSS

Wandering albatrosses only come ashore to breed on isolated islands off the coasts of Antarctica. They spend the rest of their lives in flight. These amazing birds have wingspans of up to 3.5 m, the largest of any bird. Their wings allow them to soar and glide on thermals over the Southern Ocean as they search for fish and squid. They can stay in the air for months on end, even sleeping on the wing. Using satellites to track albatross movements – a tiny satellite transmitter is fixed to a bird's body – scientists have found that an albatross can cover several thousand kilometres on a single feeding trip.

A colony of Emperor penguins with their chicks. Ungainly on land, the birds swim with ease underwater by using their flipper-like wings.

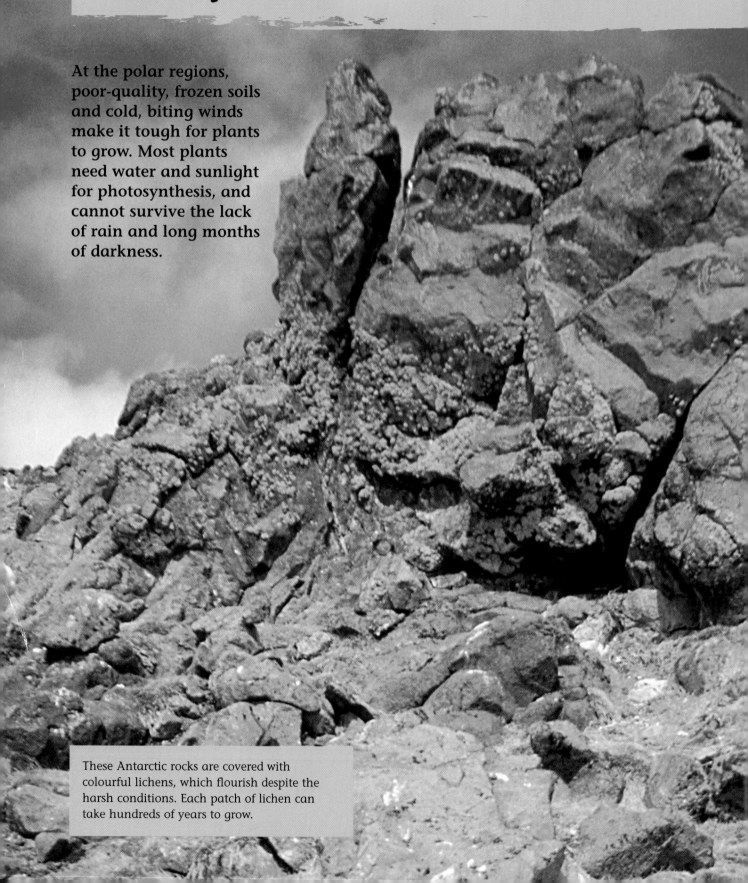

Polar plants

At the polar regions, poor-quality, frozen soils and cold, biting winds make it tough for plants to grow. Most plants need water and sunlight for photosynthesis, and cannot survive the lack of rain and long months of darkness.

These Antarctic rocks are covered with colourful lichens, which flourish despite the harsh conditions. Each patch of lichen can take hundreds of years to grow.

Despite the harsh conditions, some extremely hardy and specialized plants have adapted to life at the poles. These plants provide food for millions of insects, which spend the first part of their lives in the patches of unfrozen mud under the ice. The plants are also eaten by the large number of birds and mammals which visit the tundra during the summer months.

Arctic plants

Over a thousand species of flowering plants live on the Arctic tundra. All of them grow low to the ground to keep out of the freezing wind. Tiny trees, like Arctic willows and birches, grow sideways along the ground for many metres but never become taller than ankle height. Arctic plants grow very slowly to save energy. Pencil-thin willow stems may be hundreds of years old.

In winter, the tundra may look bare and empty. But as soon as spring comes, it bursts into life. To take advantage of the short growing season, many plants speed up their life cycles in spring and summer. While the weather is warmer and the days are longer and lighter, they flower very quickly and produce seeds and berries.

Antarctic plants

Antarctica's extreme conditions mean that only the hardiest plants can live on land. Just two species of flowering plant survive on the Antarctic Peninsula. But over 400 species of lichen have been found in the few ice-free patches of rocks or ground. Lichens have various ways of coping with the darkness and cold. Some are black for absorbing as much heat as possible from the little light available (see page 5). They also grow very slowly, since there may be only a few days in the year when conditions are suitable for growth. It can take a lichen more than 100 years to cover a patch of rock the size of a postage stamp. Some lichens can survive for over 2,000 years.

The Antarctic ice sheet itself is almost bare, although some types of algae grow on the snowfields near the coast. The algae contain a red pigment, which acts like a sunscreen to filter out the Sun's harmful ultraviolet (UV) rays and colours the snow pink. Some algae have tiny, thread-like structures for moving through the snow. They stop just below the surface, where they can collect the right amount of light to make food.

GONDWANA

Scientists have found fossils of tropical plants in Antarctica which show that it was once a much warmer place. Fossils of a conifer called *Glossopteris* have been found in Antarctica, Africa, South America, Australia and India. Until about 160 million years ago, these continents were joined together as part of a super-continent called Gondwana. Over the next 100 million years, Gondwana broke up and the continents moved apart and into their present positions. Antarctica slowly drifted towards the South Pole and got much colder. At this time, its enormous ice sheets began to form.

Life in the polar seas

Although they are very cold, the seas around the polar regions teem with life. In spring, as the ice starts to melt, vast numbers of tiny plants, called phytoplankton, bloom in the sea.

The loss of ice cover allows sunlight to reach the plants so that they can photosynthesize. The water is also rich in nutrients which the plants need to grow. The plants are grazed by tiny animals, called zooplankton, which in turn are eaten by an astonishing variety of animals, from squid and other invertebrates to fish, seals, penguins and whales.

In cold water

For animals that live in the polar oceans, keeping warm is vital. An animal's cells contain water. If this freezes, it stops the cells from working properly, damages tissues and causes death. Beneath the pack ice, the sea stays unfrozen all year round and the temperature does not change much. Krill and other invertebrates that live in the sea are therefore protected from freezing – unless they get trapped in the ice. Fish are more at risk. Seawater freezes at about –1.8°C; a fish's body fluids freeze at –1.1°C. Many Antarctic fish have a chemical, like anti-freeze, in their blood which lowers their freezing point to a safer –2°C.

Giants of the cold

The behaviour of many animals is affected by the cold of the oceans and the fact that food is scarce for most of the year. Many of the invertebrates which live on the bottom of the Southern Ocean grow and move very slowly, to save energy. Some of these

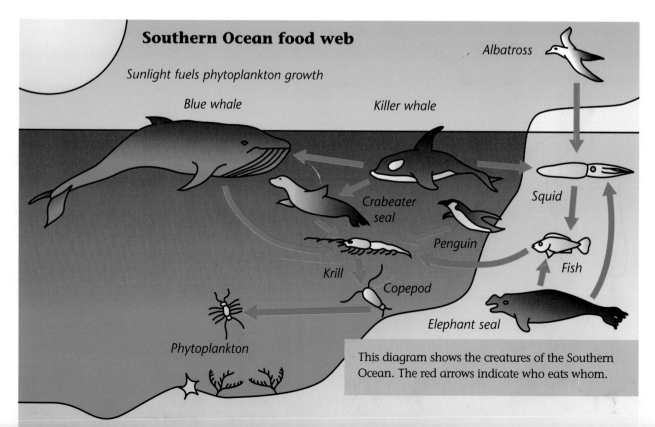

Southern Ocean food web

Sunlight fuels phytoplankton growth

Albatross

Blue whale

Killer whale

Crabeater seal

Squid

Penguin

Krill

Fish

Copepod

Elephant seal

Phytoplankton

This diagram shows the creatures of the Southern Ocean. The red arrows indicate who eats whom.

A DIET OF KRILL

Krill are shrimp-like crustaceans, found in huge swarms in the Southern Ocean. They play a crucial part in the Southern Ocean food web and are the staple diet of many fish, seals, birds and whales. The krill feed on phytoplankton growing on the underside of the pack ice. It is estimated that the Southern Ocean contains about 400 to 650 million tonnes of krill. Seals eat the most krill, about 130 million tonnes a year. Whales eat about 60 million tonnes. Krill is so important to the well-being of the Southern Ocean wildlife that scientists use radar and satellites to track and monitor the size and location of krill swarms.

creatures reach an unusually large size. A relative of the common woodlouse, *Glyptonotus* is a crustacean, which scavenges for food on the seabed. It grows up to 20 cm long, over ten times as long as an ordinary woodlouse.

A seal's life

Seals are well suited for life in the polar seas. They have streamlined bodies and paddle-like flippers for swimming, and thick layers of fat under their skin for warmth. The Weddell seal of Antarctica lives farther south than any other mammal in the world. It is also one of the hardiest. In summer, the seal breeds on the sea ice and islands around Antarctica. It spends the winter under the ice, searching for fish and squid to eat. It gnaws breathing holes in the ice with its large teeth. Underwater, a seal can hold its breath for an hour and dive to depths of over 300 m.

Weddell seals have a thick layer of insulating blubber beneath their skins to keep out the cold.

Poles under threat

Today, the polar regions are under threat. Human activities, such as mining, drilling for oil and overfishing, are putting pressure on the poles and damaging these fragile habitats.

The landscape, people, plants and animals of the poles have existed side by side for centuries. But both the Arctic and Antarctica are extremely sensitive environments. Even the slightest changes could upset the delicate, natural balance.

Global warming

Many scientists now think that the Earth is getting warmer because of the "greenhouse effect". The burning of fossil fuels, such as oil, gas and coal, is raising the amount of carbon dioxide in the atmosphere. Small amounts of carbon dioxide and other "greenhouse" gases, such as methane, occur naturally in the atmosphere. They play a vital role in trapping the Sun's heat, like the panes of glass in a greenhouse, and stopping it from escaping into space. But with the increase in carbon dioxide, the Earth is getting too warm. Not all scientists agree. Some argue that the Earth is getting warmer because of natural changes in the climate.

Impact on the ice

Scientists predict that the Earth's temperature may rise by about 2°C by the year 2100. Even this small increase could have devastating effects. Already the polar ice sheets are shrinking and some Antarctic ice shelves are breaking up. Many glaciers have started to melt and retreat. The pack ice around the Arctic has got thinner. Some studies predict that the Arctic Ocean will be completely free of summer ice before the end of the 21st century. If the polar ice melted completely, sea levels would rise by 50 m or more. This would be catastrophic, causing the flooding of low-lying coastal communities around the world.

Some scientists argue that, instead of the ice melting, the opposite will happen. They say that if the climate gets warmer, the warm air will carry more moisture to Antarctica. It will fall as rain or snow and make the ice sheet thicker.

THE OZONE LAYER

In the 1980s, scientists in Antarctica discovered a huge hole in the ozone layer. This is a layer of ozone gas about 25 km above the Earth. It shields the Earth from the Sun's harmful UV rays, which can cause skin cancer and blindness in humans and kill animals and plants. Similar holes have also been found over the Arctic region and are being carefully monitored.

The main cause of the problem are gases called CFCs. They are used in fridges, air-conditioning, plastic foam and aerosol sprays. Today, many governments have taken measures to ban CFCs. But these gases take a long time to disappear from the atmosphere and it will take another 50 to 100 years for the ozone layer to recover.

Habitat loss

If the climate changes and the polar ice continues to melt, much of the polar habitat will be lost with terrible consequences for the regions' wildlife. If plants and animals cannot adapt to the changing conditions, they will die out. Polar bears, for example, travel vast distances on floes of Arctic sea ice when they go hunting for seals. But now that the sea ice is melting earlier in the year, the bears have less time for hunting and for building up the fat stores they need to survive the winter when food is scarce. The danger is that the bears will starve.

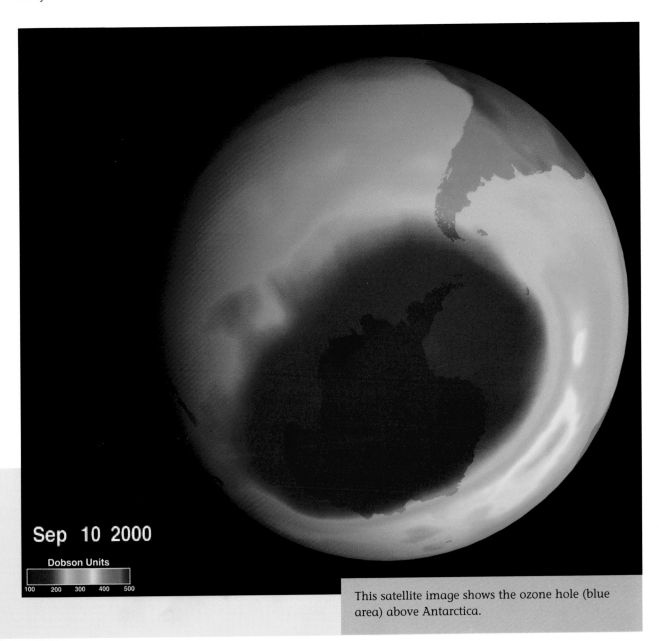

Sep 10 2000

Dobson Units

100   200   300   400   500

This satellite image shows the ozone hole (blue area) above Antarctica.

Drilling for oil

Commercial mining is banned in Antarctica until 2041, but in the Arctic things are very different. In the 1960s, oil was discovered at Prudhoe Bay in Alaska and the 1,300-km-long Trans-Alaska pipeline was built to transport the oil to the port of Valdez. The region now produces about a fifth of the USA's oil, and oil companies are looking for new supplies.

Recently, the US government announced plans to drill for oil in the Arctic National Wildlife Refuge. Covering 3 million hectares of north-east Alaska, the refuge is one of the last unspoilt areas of wilderness on Earth. It is home to huge herds of caribou and other species, including polar bears, wolves and Arctic foxes. It is also an important stop-over for many migrating birds. Environmentalists fear that drilling will damage this amazing habitat for ever. Roads, pipelines, airstrips and power stations will have to be built, displacing animals, damaging plants and disrupting the lives of local people.

Polar pollution

Pollution is another major threat to the polar regions. In 1989, the oil tanker *Exxon Valdez* ran aground off Alaska, spilling 50 million litres of oil into Prince William Sound. Hundreds of kilometres of coastline were drenched in oil and thousands of seabirds, fish and sea mammals killed. It was one of the worst environmental disasters ever.

Accidents also happen in Antarctica. In 1989, a supply ship called the *Bahia Paraiso* struck rocks off the Antarctica Peninsula. Its cargo of over 1 million litres of fuel leaked into the sea, forming a huge slick. The remote location made the clean-up campaign even more difficult.

Scientists studying the Arctic are also worried about the effect of pollution from factory chemicals and farm pesticides on local wildlife. These chemicals contaminate soils and seawater, poisoning the food chain. Rare beluga whales live in the Arctic Ocean. Already endangered, they are now under even greater threat. Many are dying

The building of pipelines, such as this one in Alaska, can result in damage to the fragile Arctic ecosystem.

POLAR TOURISM

Every year, thousands of tourists head for the poles to enjoy the breathtaking scenery and unique wildlife. Even though numbers are still low, tourists can threaten the fragile environment by leaving litter and disturbing wildlife habitats. If tourists get too close to penguins and other seabirds, it may upset the birds' breeding and nesting patterns. There are now strict rules for tourists to follow in both the Arctic and Antarctic. But polar tourism is not all negative. When they return home, polar tourists can help to improve general awareness of how precious the polar regions are.

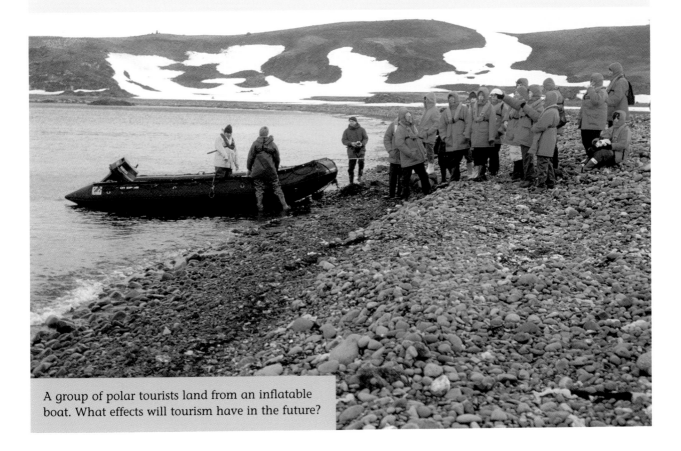

A group of polar tourists land from an inflatable boat. What effects will tourism have in the future?

of cancer and it seems that deadly chemicals washed into the sea may be to blame. These are taken in by the invertebrates on which the whales feed.

Exploiting ocean resources

Among the most important natural resources of the polar regions are fish, squid and krill. Millions of tonnes are caught each year by high-tech fleets, equipped with computers, satellites and radar for locating fish. Strict limits have been set on the size of catches to prevent overfishing. But some fishing fleets are breaking the rules. In the Southern Ocean, for example, huge numbers of the Patagonian toothfish are being caught illegally. Their oily, white meat makes them a valuable catch. The problem is that these slow-growing fish take 30 years to reach adult size. So many are being taken that the fish do not have time to breed, grow and build up stocks again.

What's being done?

There is still a great deal that we don't know about how the polar regions work. Many scientists, conservation groups and governments are working hard to learn more about the poles. All agree that it is vital to protect these fragile habitats and their unique wildlife for the future.

Science in the freezer

No one lives permanently in Antarctica, but thousands of scientists from all over the world travel there to work. They live mostly on research stations, equipped with science laboratories, living quarters, kitchens, hospitals, libraries and gyms. The scientists also spend weeks away from these stations on field trips. Many different types of scientific research are carried out. Glaciologists monitor the extent of the ice. Biologists study how wildlife adapts to the harsh climate. Geologists explore the land under the ice, and meteorologists monitor weather conditions. Antarctica's clear skies also make it a perfect place for astronomy.

There are many research stations in the Arctic. Scientists focus on environmental issues, such as the effects of pollution and climate change on the region's local people and wildlife. Projects have included the International Tundra Experiment (ITEX), which investigated the possible impact of global warming on the plants of the Arctic tundra.

Studying the ice

Because of concerns over climate change, glaciologists specialize in studying the polar ice. They use many cutting-edge techniques, such as ice-penetrating radar, lasers and satellite images to monitor changes in the thickness and extent of the ice, and in the height and speed of glaciers.

In the Arctic, submarines travelling under the sea ice have collected information about tens of thousands of square kilometres of ice, including data about its thickness and structure. Until recently, however, the Antarctic sea ice was largely unexplored.

Scientists conduct polar research at remote stations such as this one in Antarctica.

DIVING FOR SCIENCE

Scientists are constantly searching for new approaches to their work. In 2003, a team of Norwegian and British researchers used a group of white whales to collect information from the Arctic Ocean. Because of the thick ice cover, it is difficult to monitor the area by ship. The whales dive to great depths of over 200 m to feed so the scientists fitted sensors to the animals' backs. Each time the whales resurfaced, data from the sensors was sent by satellite to the researchers. Scientists are using the information to monitor the temperature of the water under the ice and to see if it is affected by global warming.

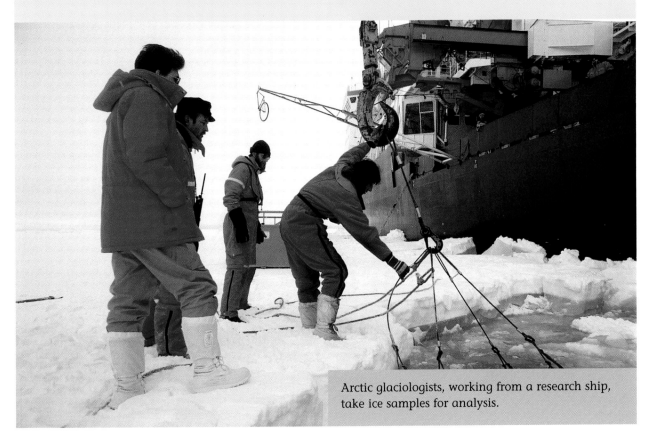

Arctic glaciologists, working from a research ship, take ice samples for analysis.

Then, in late 2003, a brand-new roving submersible, *Autosub 2*, was launched under the Antarctic sea ice. It fires sonar pulses upwards to measure the thickness of the ice.

Ice cores

The ice sheets over Greenland and the Antarctic have taken thousands of years to form. By drilling down into the ice and removing a core, scientists can tell how old the ice is. An ice core drilled recently in Antarctica was over 3 km long and the ice at the bottom almost one million years old. Ice cores are extremely valuable. Locked in the ice is a unique record of past climate change. As the ice forms, particles of dust or pollen get trapped inside it. By analyzing these gases and particles, scientists can work out what the Earth's climate and atmosphere were like in the past. The ice also provides information about past events, such as volcanic eruptions. The results are helping scientists to predict how the climate might change in the future.

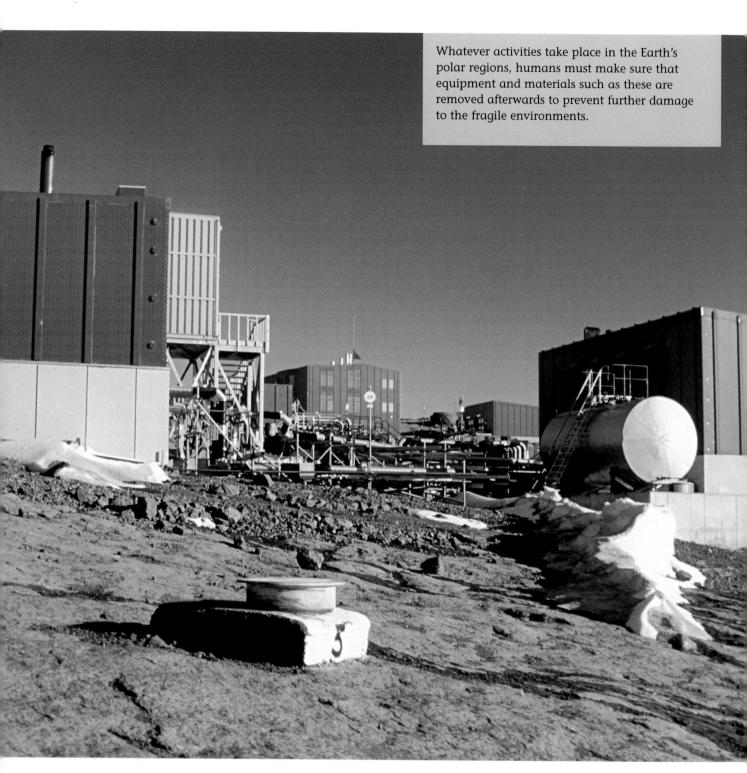

Whatever activities take place in the Earth's polar regions, humans must make sure that equipment and materials such as these are removed afterwards to prevent further damage to the fragile environments.

Conservation at work

Environmental groups are working hard to save the polar regions. In the 1980s, Greenpeace began a long-running campaign to protect the Antarctic region. Greenpeace was worried about the environmental damage caused by the scientific bases. Problems included dumping sewage and chemicals into the sea, burning rubbish, and blasting wildlife sites to make room for buildings and airstrips. Thanks to pressure from Greenpeace, the bases have now cleaned up their act. Many have strict waste management programmes and specially trained environment officers. Rubbish is no longer burned or dumped but recycled or shipped home.

In the Arctic, the WWF (Worldwide Fund for Nature) began its International Arctic Programme in 1992 as a joint effort between the eight Arctic countries. Its aim is to protect the Arctic from further damage and to make the rest of the world aware of how important the region is. Among other things, the WWF is working to find ways of reducing pollution, saving local wildlife, and protecting the rights and culture of local Arctic people.

Saving living resources

In the 19th and early 20th centuries, hunters came to Antarctica in search of whales and seals. Sealers came especially to hunt fur seals for their valuable pelts and elephant seals for their blubber. By the 1920s, both species were almost extinct. The whales of the Southern Ocean suffered a similar fate. As whale stocks were wiped out in other oceans, whalers moved further south. Millions of whales were killed for their

blubber, whalebone and meat. In 1994, the International Whaling Commission (IWC) declared the Southern Ocean a whale sanctuary. Whales are now protected from commercial hunting, although a few are still caught for scientific research. Seals are also protected by the Convention for the Conservation of Antarctic Seals.

In both polar regions, certain areas have been set aside as protected parks. The world's largest national park covers 972,000 sq km of north-eastern Greenland. It is home to polar bears, caribou, musk oxen and many rare Arctic plants. Seals, whales and walruses live around the coasts.

New parks are being set up. In January 2004, Australia established a fully-protected marine reserve in its Antarctic waters. The reserve covers an area about one-and-a-half times the size of Switzerland and includes a group of remote islands which are home to several threatened species. To safeguard these animals and their habitat, commercial fishing and exploration will in future be banned in the new reserve and only a limited amount of carefully-monitored scientific research will be allowed.

THE FUTURE

What does the future hold for the polar regions? Already, there are many treaties and measures in place to protect these amazing habitats. But should they remain protected areas set aside for peaceful, scientific research? Or should they be developed like other parts of the world? Parts of the Arctic have already been developed, and the Antarctic may follow. Recently scientists began calling for tighter rules to control the collecting of biological samples which could be used by commercial companies. These include a type of protein

used by certain kinds of Antarctic bacteria as an anti-freeze. It could be used to keep frozen foods fresher for longer and so would be very valuable to food companies. In the Arctic, governments are trying to find ways of developing the region without causing more damage to the fragile ecosystem. At the other end of the Earth, many people believe that the best way to protect Antarctica is to turn it into a world park where any commercial activity is completely banned. Whether either of these plans will work remains to be seen.

Further information

International agreements

The Antarctic

In addition to the Antarctic Treaty, four international agreements have been made to tackle environmental problems. Here are the main points of each agreement:

1. (1964) Agreed Measures for the Conservation of Antarctic Fauna and Flora. (Many of these measures have been updated in the Environmental Protocol.)
- Killing or catching any bird or mammal without a permit is forbidden.
- Permits will only be given for scientific samples and essential food.
- Vehicles and explosives must not be used near wildlife colonies.
- Some areas will be Specially Protected Areas.
- Non-indigenous species are not allowed without a permit.

2. (1972) Convention for the Conservation of Antarctic Seals (CCAS)
- Yearly catches are strictly controlled and reviewed regularly.
- Killing of Ross and Antarctic fur seals is banned.
- Killing of any seals between March-August is banned.
- Killing of any seals in special reserves is banned.

3. (1982) Convention on the Conservation of Antarctic Marine Living Resources (CCAS)
- Applies to fish, molluscs, crustaceans and all other species, including birds, which form part of the Antarctic marine ecosystem.
- Any harvesting of resources must follow strict conservation measures:

- Stocks must not fall below certain levels.
- A balance must be kept between resources caught and those that depend on them for food.
- No long-term changes must be made to the marine ecosystem.
- Conservation measures must be followed.
- A special scientific committee will give advice about these measures.

4. (1998) Protocol on Environmental Protection to the Antarctic Treaty
- Sets aside Antarctica as a natural reserve devoted to peace and science.
- Sets out rules to protect the environment.
- Gives priority to scientific research.
- Bans all activities relating to mineral resources (apart from scientific research).
- Sets out rules for:
  • Environmental impact of activities
  • Conservation of flora and fauna
  • Waste disposal and management
  • Prevention of marine pollution
  • Special area protection and management
- Bans non-indigenous species without a permit.

The Arctic

The Arctic Council

In the Arctic, the land is owned by the eight Arctic countries – Canada, Denmark/Greenland, Finland, Iceland, Norway, Russia, Sweden and the USA. Their governments have joined forces to form the Arctic Council and are working together to protect the Arctic region.

Arctic Council Agreements

The Arctic Council has put in place various programmes and measures to safeguard the Arctic environment.

1. Arctic Monitoring and Assessment Programme (AMAP)
   Monitors pollution in the Arctic and looks at its causes and at its impact on the environment. Also looks at international agreements on pollution control.
2. Protection of the Arctic Marine Environment (PAME)
   Looks at ways of preventing pollution of the Arctic marine environment from land and sea-based activities, such as shipping, oil and gas exploration and ocean dumping.
3. Conservation of Arctic Flora and Fauna (CAFF)
   Aims to protect Arctic species and to regulate how they are harvested and used, to prevent overfishing and so on. Looks at how climate change affects Arctic wildlife and how wildlife is adapting to the changes.
4. Emergency, Prevention, Preparedness and Response (EPPR)
   Exchanges information about how best to prevent oil and chemical spills in Arctic waters and how to act quickly if a spill occurs.
5. The Arctic Climate Change Impact Assessment (ACIA)
   Runs projects to assess how much the Arctic is warming up and the impact of future climate change on the region, its wildlife and people, as well as possible measures to take.

Websites

Here are a few websites to help you to find out more about the polar regions:

www.antarctica.ac.uk
The website of the British Antarctic Survey with information and scientists' diaries.

http://astro.uchicago.edu/cara/vtour/mcmurdo
A virtual tour of the USA's McMurdo base in Antarctica.

http://usarc.usgs.gov
The website of the US Antarctic Resource Center with a huge collection of maps, photos and information.

www.spri.cam.ac.uk
The Scott Polar Research Institute website with information about the Arctic, its people, landscape and wildlife.

www.arctic-council.org
The website of the Arctic Council which is made up of the Arctic countries.

www.ngo.grida.no/wwfap
The website of the WWF Arctic Programme with details of current projects, including tracking polar bears.

www.glacier.rice.edu
Facts, figures and maps about conditions in the Arctic and Antarctica.

www.iaato.org
The website of the International Association of Antarctica Tour Operators with information about tourism.

Glossary

Adapted
Having certain features or ways of behaving which allow a plant or animal to survive in a particular habitat.

Albedo effect
The way in which dark colours absorb, or soak up, heat and light colours reflect it away.

Algae
A group of simple plants, ranging from tiny, one-celled plants to huge seaweeds.

Antarctic Circle
An imaginary circle drawn around the southernmost part of the Earth.

Arctic Circle
An imaginary circle drawn around the northernmost part of the Earth.

Axis
An imaginary line drawn through the middle of the Earth, between the North and South Poles.

Bacteria
Microscopic, single-celled living things found almost everywhere.

Blubber
A thick layer of fat under an animal's skin.

Carbon dioxide
A gas found in the atmosphere. It is released when fuel, such as coal or wood, burns and when animals breathe out.

CFCs
Gases, called chlorofluorocarbons, which are destroying the ozone layer above the poles.

Crustaceans
Animals, such as krill, shrimps and crabs.

Dry valleys
Areas of bare rock in Antarctica which are not covered in ice and snow.

Ecosystem
A community of animals and plants and the habitat they live in.

Food chains
The way in which living things are linked together by what they eat.

Food web
A number of different food chains linked together.

Geology
The study of the Earth's structure.

Glaciologists
Scientists who study ice.

Ice cap
A vast covering of ice over land.

Invertebrates
Animals which do not have backbones or skeletons inside their bodies.

Meteorologists
Scientists who study weather and climate.

Migration
The journeys undertaken by some animals between different habitats, at different times of the year.

Nutrients
Substances in food that plants and animals need to stay alive.

Ozone layer
A layer of ozone gas in the Earth's atmosphere that protects living things from the Sun's harmful UV rays.

Photosynthesis
The process by which green plants make their food from carbon dioxide and water, using energy from sunlight.

Phytoplankton
Microscopic, single-celled plants which drift in the sea and begin the ocean food chain.

Protein
A chemical substance, which a living thing needs for healthy growth.

Sonar pulses
Bleeps of sound used to measure the thickness of the polar ice.

Tundra
The area of flat, treeless land around the Arctic Ocean where only low plants and shrubs can grow.

UV (ultraviolet) rays
Harmful rays from the Sun that are invisible to the human eye. They can cause cancer and blindness in humans and kill animals and plants.

Wind-chill factor
The way in which the wind makes it feel colder than it actually is. The stronger the wind, the colder it feels.

Zooplankton
Tiny sea animals which graze on phytoplankton.

Index